THE CRIMES OF ISIS

ISIS BRIDES

Bridey Heing

Enslow Publishing

101 W. 23rd Street
Suite 240
New York, NY 10011
USA

enslow.com

Published in 2018 by Enslow Publishing, LLC.
101 W. 23rd Street, Suite 240, New York, NY 10011

Library of Congress Cataloging-in-Publication Data

Names: Heing, Bridey, author.
Title: ISIS brides / by Bridey Heing.
Description: New York, NY : Enslow Publishing, 2018. | Series: The crimes of
  ISIS | Includes bibliographical references and index. | Audience: Grades 7–12.
Identifiers: LCCN 2017019582 | ISBN 9780766092136 (library bound) | ISBN
  9780766095823 (paperback)
Subjects: LCSH: IS (Organization)—Juvenile literature. | Women terrorists—
  Juvenile literature. | Terrorism—Religious aspects—Islam—Juvenile literature. |
  Women—Violence against—Islamic countries—Juvenile literature. | Women—
  Abuse of—Islamic countries—Juvenile literature. | Human trafficking—Islamic
  countries—Juvenile literature.
Classification: LCC HV6433.I722 H453 2018 | DDC 363.325082/091767—dc23
LC record available at https://lccn.loc.gov/2017019582

Printed in the United States of America

To Our Readers: We have done our best to make sure all website addresses in this
book were active and appropriate when we went to press. However, the author and
the publisher have no control over and assume no liability for the material available
on those websites or on any websites they may link to. Any comments or suggestions
can be sent by email to customerservice@enslow.com.

CONTENTS

INTRODUCTION

In 2013, a little-known Muslim extremist organization shocked the world when it began taking control of huge areas of Iraq and Syria. The Islamic State in Iraq and Syria, better known by the acronym ISIS, has since proven to be one of the most barbaric and violent terrorist organizations operating today, killing thousands of people and inspiring vicious, violent attacks around the world. Known as much for its well-documented violence as for its ability to find supporters through social media, ISIS is one of the greatest problems facing the international community.

Stories of women are among the most confusing and harrowing of those told about ISIS. From the women who are kidnapped and forced into marriage with ISIS fighters to the young women who leave their home countries to voluntarily join the group, women are at the heart of some of the most controversial facets of ISIS's rise to and hold on power. The group's

A woman in India wears a traditional Muslim niqab, a head scarf that covers the entire head and face, leaving only the wearer's eyes visible. The niqab is typically worn in public or in front of men who are not family.

ideology is rooted in the oppression of women, who are seen as serving only one purpose: that of mothers and caretakers for their husbands.

ISIS is a group dominated by men. Women are confined to the home and expected to be covered from head to toe when in public. Marriage and having children—who will go on to be the next generation of ISIS fighters—is the utmost duty any woman can have, along with taking care of her fighter husband and remarrying quickly when he is killed in battle. Although it promotes itself as truly pro-women and allowing women to live devout lives, in truth, ISIS uses abuse and terror to control women's every choice, even using female enforcers to keep other women under control.

Thousands of women live in ISIS territory, including hundreds who have traveled from around the world to marry fighters and thousands who have been abducted and forced to become slaves or wives. The group has become adept at recruiting women via social media, encouraging them to travel to Syria to marry fighters and support their cause, and to help them build a functioning state in the rapidly diminishing territory they hold. While many women are caught trying to do so by authorities, many others are able to cross the border into Syria, where they help recruit other women from around the world.

All of these women are, to varying degrees, oppressed by ISIS's teachings; women are discouraged from leaving the house alone, holding jobs, continuing education past an early age, or disobeying their husbands. While some have reportedly had warm marriages, far more have endured abuse at the hands of the men they married either voluntarily or by force, with some being bought and sold like objects to various men in cities across ISIS territory.

But women are also on the forefront when it comes to fighting ISIS. They undermine ISIS's rule by helping women escape their territory, lead groups that provide services to women who have fled, engage in direct combat against ISIS forces to retake territory, and advocate for prosecution of ISIS leaders on the international stage. Even as ISIS has worked tirelessly to control women, women have worked tirelessly to bring the group to justice and save all the people who continue to live in fear under ISIS rule.

A HISTORY OF
ISIS

In late 2013, ISIS made headlines around the world when it took control of Fallujah, Iraq. It seemed that the group had appeared overnight and was unstoppable as it conquered villages and broadcast its violence over the internet while calling out Western powers and regional states alike. In the years since, its power has ebbed and flowed, but it remains the most attention-grabbing and influential terrorist organization in the world.

But ISIS had existed in varying forms long before 2013. The group may have made headlines that year, but it had been setting the groundwork for its rapid rise to power since 2004. Although early on the group was part of al-Qaeda's network of affiliates, it soon became clear that the group that would become ISIS was of a different sort altogether, with plans far more heinous than any al-Qaeda had imagined.

AL-QAEDA IN IRAQ

ISIS's roots can be traced back to 2004, when Abu Musab al-Zarqawi started an insurgent group in Iraq pledged

In June 2014, in Mosul, Iraq, ISIS supporters march and chant pro-ISIS slogans while carrying the flag of the Islamic State. Although the majority of Muslims around the world condemn ISIS for their barbaric beliefs and use of violence, the group has still managed to find supporters in Iraq and Syria—and around the world.

to al-Qaeda. He had been leading attacks against US forces there, but his popularity started dwindling among fighters when he began attacking Muslims. Just two years after pledging his allegiance to Osama bin Laden, al-Zarqawi was killed in a US airstrike and was replaced as head of al-Qaeda in Iraq by Abu Ayyub al-Masri. In late 2006, al-Masri announced the formation of the Islamic State of Iraq (ISI) and named Abu Omar al-Baghdadi as a coleader. The move was a rebranding attempt after the popularity of al-Qaeda began to diminish in Iraq, but the group remained loyal to al-Qaeda.

Abu Musab al-Zarqawi, the leader of al-Qaeda in Iraq, the predecesor to ISIS, is shown holding a machine gun in this still from a video shot in 2006.

Until 2009, ISI was not a powerful group in the region. It had few members, and thousands of its fighters had been captured by Iraqi and US forces. But the group was known for brutality even then, and for its extreme fanaticism. Under al-Zarqawi, the group had established itself as willing to kill other Muslims or excommunicate them for infractions such as shaving or voting. This extremism continued even as its numbers dwindled to a few thousand in 2008.

But the tide turned in its favor when, in 2009, Shiite prime minister of Iraq Nouri al-Maliki was seen as favoring Shiites over Sunnis, who started to feel disenfranchised and ignored by the government. ISI was able to play on that sense of isolation to gain followers, particularly in rural and tribal areas, as it started carrying out terrorist attacks in Baghdad. Although still a marginal group, it marked a turning point for ISI and created a stronger base of support that was inherited the next year by a little-known extremist named Abu Bakr al-Baghdadi.

ABU BAKR AL-BAGHDADI

Abu Bakr al-Baghdadi, born Ibrahim Ibrahim Awad Ibrahim al-Badri, is largely a mystery. He has been described by former peers as a quiet and isolated student who never made much of an impression. He earned multiple degrees in Islamic studies from schools in Baghdad, although it is disputed at which school he earned his PhD. He became a militant after 2003 and was arrested by US forces in 2004, but he was released later that year after being labeled a "low level prisoner." An anonymous Pentagon official familiar with his detention told the *New York Times* that he was "a street thug" at the time of his arrest and said, "It's hard to imagine we could have had a crystal ball then that would tell us he'd become head of ISIS."[1]

ISIS leader Abu Bakr al-Baghdadi is shown here in a mugshot from 2004, when he was detained at Camp Bucca in Iraq after being detained by US armed forces.

Al-Baghdadi took over leadership of ISI in 2010, after al-Masri and Abu Omar al-Baghdadi were killed in US-Iraqi operations. He moved quickly to carry out large-scale attacks, and in 2011, ISI claimed responsibility for suicide bombings in Baghdad and the city's surrounding area. That year, al-Baghdadi also helped create al-Nusra Front, a Syria-based al-Qaeda affiliate that was established after the outbreak of the civil war there. The wave of violence continued in 2012, as ISI, under al-Baghdadi, began freeing prisoners who had been arrested while members of al-Qaeda in Iraq.

In 2013, al-Baghdadi began consolidating his power. By that point, a rift had formed between him and al-Qaeda leadership, largely over tactics. While al-Qaeda's willingness to kill civilians has been one of its hallmarks, ISI surpassed it in cruelty and barbaric violence, as well as willingness to kill and excommunicate fellow Muslims, something al-Qaeda did not agree with. Those tensions reached a head when Raqqa, Syria, fell to a variety of opposition groups, including both ISI and al-Nusra Front. Shortly after Raqqa fell, al-Baghdadi announced that ISI would become known as the Islamic State in Iraq and Syria (or al-Sham), shortened to ISIS, and that al-Nusra Front was joining the group. This attempt to absorb al-Nusra Front was rebuffed by the group's leader, Abu Mohammed al-Jawlani, and al-Nusra remains loyal to al-Qaeda.

Between April 2013 and June 2014, ISIS moved fast to take a large swath of territory in Syria and Iraq. At one point, the group was within a few hundred miles of Baghdad, with control of Mosul and Tikrit in Iraq. In early 2014, al-Qaeda announced that it was cutting ties with ISIS, and ISIS began forcing all other militant groups out of Raqqa, which it made its headquarters. By mid-2014, al-Baghdadi was ready to declare his state.

ISIS DECLARES A CALIPHATE

In June 2014, al-Baghdadi announced the formation of a caliphate under the name Islamic State. This is not a name generally used by media and officials, out of respect to the fact that the vast majority of Muslims do not recognize the validity of al-Baghdadi's so-called government.

The term "caliphate" comes from the earliest days of the Islamic Empire, when a caliph, or religious leader, governed most of the world's Muslim community. There is some controversy in Muslim history about the nature and validity of caliphate rule; only two caliphs were ever recognized by both Sunnis and Shiites. The last caliphate was the Ottoman Empire, which governed most of the Middle East and parts of Africa until 1924. The caliph is both a religious and a political leader who oversees the running of the territorial state and guides Muslims. By declaring his territory a caliphate, al-Baghdadi has positioned himself as the supposed leader of all Muslims and declared that it is the responsibility of all Muslims to pledge their allegiance to him and to ISIS.

This has not happened, and only a small number of Muslims from around the world have traveled to Syria to live under al-Baghdadi's rule. Those who have joined have contributed to a global concern about the ability of ISIS to recruit from abroad and fears that fighters could return to their home countries to carry out attacks. This has been exacerbated by attacks in Paris and Belgium, where ISIS-inspired and -aligned terrorists have carried out complex attacks against civilians.

LIFE UNDER AL-BAGHDADI

In ISIS territory, al-Baghdadi and his forces use terror to control the population. They are responsible for widespread ethnic

ISIS leader Abu Bakr al-Baghdadi is shown here in July 2014, during an appearance at a mosque in Mosul, Iraq. This image was captured a month after al-Baghdadi announced the formation of the caliphate, or Islamic State, and his position as caliph, or leader.

cleansing, forcing non-Sunni Muslims to convert or face death or slavery. Mass executions are carried out in public, as well as amputations meant to punish those who violate rules. Men and women alike are harshly punished for even simple infractions, while fighters and foreigners who join the group are given freedoms that others are not.

Little is known about day-to-day life under ISIS, but what is known suggests that the group is trying to function like a state, albeit an oppressive one. Everything from marriage to

HIJAB

Millions of women around the world wear hijab when they leave their homes, a sign of modesty that is taught in Islam. For most of them, it is a personal choice they make to express their faith, but in some places, such as Iran and Saudi Arabia, hijab is mandatory for women in public. Hijab refers to a wide range of coverings women wear, from the simple headscarf that can be worn to cover hair to the full abaya and niqab, which covers the entire body and face. ISIS requires that women wear the abaya, a black dress that drapes loosely, and the niqab, which covers the head and face with just a small opening through which to see. Some women also wear black gloves so that no skin is showing. The abaya cannot be too tight; it cannot show the shape of the body at all. Women who do not closely follow these requirements face harassment and beatings by the authorities. Although women who choose to wear hijab in its many forms are making a free decision, women under ISIS are forced by the group to undertake this practice.

slavery is carefully institutionalized and governed by rules, documentation, and other trappings of bureaucracy. Leaked documents from inside the group's governing apparatus suggest that it has struggled to meet its own financial obligations, and wages to fighters have been cut as oil revenue and other sources of income have diminished along with its territory.

Among stories from those who have survived living under ISIS, "fear" is perhaps the most common word used to describe their existences. Life is dominated by violent spectacle and the threat that someone could turn you in for wearing makeup or listening to the radio. One man living in Raqqa told the *Guardian* in 2015 that the city was "a giant prison,"[2] where personal freedoms are heavily curtailed. Employment opportunities are few, and some are obligated to join ISIS in exchange for a small amount of money to support their families. Social media posts from within ISIS territory, though largely upbeat, allude to electricity being scarce and intermittent access to the internet for those who are fortunate enough to be allowed online.

AN IDEOLOGY OF VIOLENCE

ISIS's ideology is rooted in Salafism, an extremely conservative school of Sunni thought that emerged in the eighteenth century in response to European colonialism. Salafist leaders believed that Muslims should live more in accordance with traditional ways of life rather than "Westernized" modernity. This fundamentalist outlook has kept Salafist teachings in the margins of Muslim society, but it, along with Wahhabism, has inspired groups like al-Qaeda, Boko Haram, and other extremist organizations around the world.

Not all followers of Salafism believe in using violence. Although their beliefs may be extreme to some, many Salafists do not advocate terrorism. When groups that are identified as Salafist take up violence as a tool, they are known as Jihadi Salafi organizations. ISIS falls into this category; it uses terrorism and violence to force people to live by a set of standards it has drawn from Islamic teachings but have adapted in arbitrary ways to meet its needs.

While most Muslims do not agree with ISIS, Bernard Haykel, a Princeton University scholar and one of the foremost experts on ISIS ideology, told the *Atlantic* that ISIS's beliefs are rooted in a close and literal reading of Islamic texts and that he feels the group is re-creating the norms of war that dominated in the time of the prophet Mohammed, around the sixth century CE. This includes crucifixion, slavery, and other practices that are widely accepted as having no place in modern society.[3] Even its language mimics the norms of that period; the group frequently uses "Rome" as a stand-in for the West in declarations of intent to conquer the rest of the world, a callback to a time when Rome was the global superpower.

ISIS hopes to use its uniquely wanton violence to establish control over the traditional Islamic Empire, a wide-ranging territory that includes much of the modern Middle East,

ISIS supporters drive around Raqqa, Syria, in June 2014, waving the flag of the caliphate weeks after Abu Bakr al-Baghdadi announced the formation of the caliphate.

North Africa, and into Turkey. The group also believes in an apocalyptic prophecy that states the end of the world will come when the armies of "Rome" are defeated by a few thousand devout followers of the caliphate at Dabiq in Syria. This millenarian ideology drives its devotion to and near worship

WAHHABISM

ISIS is a Salafist extremist group, but it is sometimes associated with Wahhabism. Like Salafism, Wahhabism emerged as a school of Sunni thought during the colonial period, and it advocates for a strict reading of the Quran and rejection of Western norms. Founded by Muhammad ibn Abd al-Wahhab, the movement shares ISIS's practice of excluding Muslims who practice things it considers impure, such as venerating saints. ISIS has not shied away from denouncing and executing fellow Muslims, a practice that most Muslims—including extremist groups— reject. Wahhabism also embraces the intense violence that ISIS uses, including assaulting and murdering women.

Wahhabism became politically important when Muhammad Ibn Saud and his followers aligned themselves with the school of thought. Ibn Saud used Wahhabist teachings as validation for his own widespread raiding and forced conversion policy, which won him great power. The House of Saud would eventually become the ruling family of Saudi Arabia in 1932, where Wahhabism is the state religion. It manifests in Saudi Arabia in restrictions of women, including prohibiting them from driving and requiring that they wear hijab. Most Muslims reject Wahhabism as too extreme, and its ties to Saudi terrorist groups like al-Qaeda have made it the focus of anti-terrorism work.

of death; the group celebrates when members die, and widowed wives are discouraged from expressing sadness or doubt over their husbands' deaths.

The place of women in this ideology that is so driven by male-centric ideas of strength is complex, but ultimately, ISIS upholds the idea that women should live in servitude to men and the state. Women are required to wear full-body and face coverings and are discouraged from leaving the house unnecessarily. Those who do not adhere to ISIS's teachings are at threat of being made slaves or sexually abused. Although women are key to promoting ISIS's vision for the future and luring in new recruits, even those who believe in ISIS's teachings are expected to sacrifice personal freedoms in the name of living a more holy life.

2

WOMEN IN

ISIS IDEOLOGY

ISIS is a predominantly male-centered group, with practices that force women into the home and guarantee them few rights. Whether as wives or slaves, women serve one purpose for ISIS, and that is reproduction. There are some regulations that are meant to govern the treatment of women, but in practice, most women living under ISIS experience a cycle of violence and abuse that ends only if they are able to escape. This is true of both Muslim women, who are offered some rights, and non-Muslim women, who are sold as slaves.

ISIS is a fairly prolific group, publishing a wide range of documents that highlight the role of women and what they are expected to do in the caliphate. Chief among their responsibilities are marriage and having children, while some can undertake jobs that fit into a narrow idea of what women should be allowed to do. Foreign women are encouraged to recruit other women, while others are allowed to teach or join the morality police. For slaves, life is a cycle of abuse during which they are sold, held captive, and sexually assaulted.

Women in Raqqa, Syria, walk past a billboard that suggests women wear traditional Islamic clothing. The billboard, put up by ISIS supporters, quotes the Quran in an effort to get Muslim women to cover themselves.

THE ROLE OF MUSLIM WOMEN

Women are central to ISIS's ideology, but not on their own merits. Women do not become leaders in ISIS, and they do not fight. Instead they are meant to support fighters and raise morale, while helping to create a functional state within the caliphate by teaching, keeping house, and having children who will be indoctrinated into ISIS's violent way of life. "The strategy is geared to building a community and bringing families in so they have the infrastructure to set up a society," Melanie Smith, research associate at the International Center for the Study of Radicalization at King's College London, told *Time*.[1] But this is true only of Muslim women—all others are considered potential slaves.

The Khansaa Brigade, ISIS's all-female morality police, published a guide that is believed to be for women living under ISIS control. The guide is called *Women of the Islamic State: Manifesto and Case Study* and is published only in Arabic, but it was translated by counterterrorism group the Quilliam Foundation. It includes ten chapters that provide rules for women to follow to live up to the Muslim woman's role in society. It also offers us an understanding of what life is like for Muslim women and what is expected of them beyond the propaganda the group uses to lure women to Syria.

Among other things, the guide decries the "liberation" of women in modern society and calls for women to be fully covered and stay in their homes. "It is always preferable for a woman to

A family fleeing Mosul, Iraq, after ISIS took control of the city in 2014 arrives at a Kurdish checkpoint in Kalak, Iraq. Thousands of familes were forced to flee their homes and seek accommodation in refugee camps after ISIS declared their caliphate.

RETAKING MOSUL

Mosul, Iraq, was one of the first conquests that pointed at what ISIS could be capable of. But in early 2017, Iraqi forces, with air support from other states, were able to largely retake the city, liberating the scores of civilians who had been living under ISIS rule since 2014. Although at the time of the writing the city was still home to groups of ISIS fighters and airstrikes were underway, the retaking of most of Mosul marked a symbolic victory over ISIS. It also gave the public an understanding of what ISIS looks like when it is on the offensive and freed many who could provide evidence of ISIS's brutal rule. But as of early 2017, around 400,000 remained in ISIS-held parts of West Mosul. The group has begun using human shields, hiding themselves among civilian populations to deter the use of airstrikes against areas of the city they hold. They are also executing anyone who tries to flee in an attempt to scare anyone else who might be thinking of doing the same. This, combined with the mass graves, makeshift prisons, and stories of widespread abuse, paints a picture of a group that will fight bitterly and horrifically until it is defeated.

remain hidden and veiled," the guide reads. Although veiling is a personal choice many women make around the world, under ISIS it is mandatory, and women who are deemed immodest run the risk of being punished with whippings. According to the Quilliam Foundation, "Women are forced to be accompanied by a man at all times and are forced to wear a double layered veil, gloves and a loose abaya [cloak]."[2]

Motherhood is the core role of women living under ISIS, and it takes precedence over any other ambition or hope she might have for her life. To this end, marriage is essentially mandatory. The guide reads that for women, "There is no responsibility greater for her than that of being a wife to her husband."

MARRIAGE IN THE CALIPHATE

For women living under ISIS rule, marriage is the prime determining factor in their lives. The man they marry will determine their status, with foreign fighters more highly ranked than local recruits, and he will be given almost complete control over her life. For some, this works out all right; there are stories of women living with men who do not abuse them or disrespect them. But for most, marriage is a kind of prison, and their husbands are free to beat or assault them as they see fit.

Dua, Aws, and Asma were living in Raqqa when ISIS took control of the city in 2014. They were among those who could join the group voluntarily, a chance that spared their lives but created new difficulties. They all began working for the Khansaa Brigade, a morality police force that patrols the streets of the city and issues punishments for infractions like improper dress or wearing makeup. Marriage to fighters is another way the women were able to stay in ISIS's good graces, as the women learned when they first married foreign fighters. But even for these young women, who were living as privileged lives as were possible for Syrians living under ISIS, life eventually became unbearable.

Marriage was initially good for the young women, but soon ISIS's oppressive views of marriage became clear. Dua and Aws both lost their husbands, who they married by choice, in suicide missions. They were both heartbroken, both by the men's deaths

An Iraqi woman who was forced to flee Mosul, Iraq, after ISIS took control of the city shows a marriage license issued by the terrorist organization.

and by the fact that they did not tell their wives about volunteering for the mission. Just days after other fighters told her about her husband's death, another came to Dua's door and informed her that she had to remarry immediately.

"I had a good marriage to a good man, and I didn't want to end up in a bad one," Dua told the *New York Times*. "I knew it would be painful for me to marry someone only to lose him when he goes on a martyrdom mission. It's only natural to have feelings and grow attached."[3]

Aws was given similar guidance. "They told me that he was a martyr now, obviously he didn't need a wife anymore, but that there was another fighter who did. They said this fighter had been my husband's friend, and wanted to protect and take care of me on his behalf," Aws told the *New York Times*.

Fear of losing their husbands is common in social media posts from ISIS brides. One woman who went to Syria from Malaysia and married a man she had never seen wrote frequently on social media in 2014 about her fears that her husband could be killed on a mission. Being widowed is a tragedy for any woman in a loving marriage, but it carries extra concern for women living under ISIS: They will be forced to remarry quickly, and their next husband might not be so kind.

THE ROLE OF NON-MUSLIM WOMEN

ISIS has made it clear that non-Muslim women have only one place in their caliphate: slavery. Its propaganda and guidance offer multiple instances of it excusing and even encouraging the enslavement and sexual assault of non-Muslim women, including children. According to the ISIS magazine *Dabiq*:

> Unlike the Jews and Christians, there was no room for jizyah (non-Muslim residents) payment. Also, their women could be enslaved... After capture, the Yazidi women and children were then divided according to the Sharī'ah10 amongst the fighters of the Islamic State who participated in the Sinjar operations, after one fifth of the slaves were transferred to the Islamic State's authority to be divided as khums [fifth]... Before Shaytān [Satan] reveals his doubts to the weak-minded and weak hearted, one should remember that enslaving the families of the kuffār [infidels] and taking their women as concubines is a firmly established aspect of the Sharī'ah...[4]

Jizyah is a Muslim system of taxation that was used during the Islamic Empire as a way for those of non-Muslim,

Abrahamic faiths to live under the Islamic rule. The tax was enshrined in the Quran, and with it came the right of Christians, Zoroastrians, and Jews to practice their faith. Although it claims to have a system of jizyah, ISIS does not; there have been numerous documented cases wherein it attacked and persecuted Christians, Jews, and even Shia Muslims who did not convert to Islam.

Another publication states, "It is permissible to buy, sell, or give as a gift female captives and slaves, for they are merely property, which can be disposed of..."[5] ISIS uses Quranic teachings that are centuries old and widely considered outdated or non-binding to govern its use of slaves, although it also twists teachings to fit its needs, as it did with the mourning period offered to widows before remarriage. Mention of slavery or treatment of slaves is not rare in religious texts; most were written at a time when slavery was common and accepted, and religious teachings were a means to create a uniform guide to treatment of slaves.

Prior to taking the Iraqi city of Sinjar, where the large Yazidi population was taken captive, ISIS organized efforts to put slavery into practice. *Dabiq* published an article called "The Revival of Slavery Before the Hour" about the efforts that October, saying that ISIS researched the Yazidi minority. According to the article, "After capture, the Yazidi women and children were then divided according to Shariah amongst the fighters of the Islamic State who participated in the Sinjar operations, after one fifth of the slaves were transferred to the Islamic State's authority to be divided."

There is some evidence, however, that the treatment of these women has caused controversy among ISIS followers. In 2015, *Dabiq* published an op-ed by a woman denouncing ISIS supporters who believed "the soldiers of the [caliphate] had

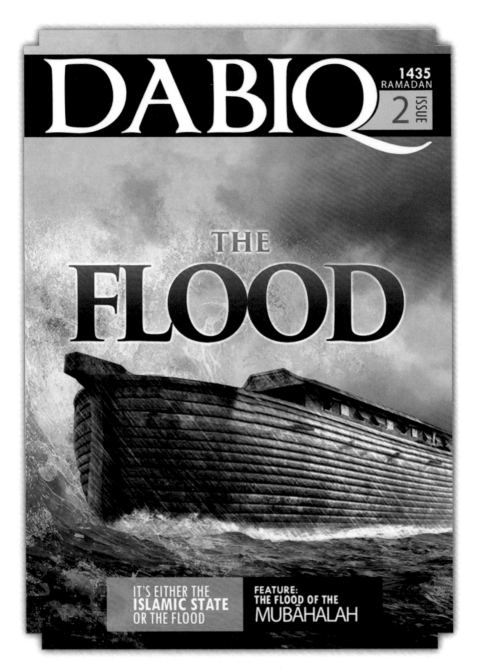

ISIS is skilled at promoting their viewpoint to Western supporters and potential converts through social media as well as through an English-language magazine, *Dabiq*.

YAZIDIS

The Yazidis are a religious minority based largely in northern Iraq. Only about 700,000 Yazidis live around the world, and it is impossible to convert to the faith. The group was heavily targeted by ISIS, which has been accused of genocide against the Yazidis. Isolated due to the close-knit nature of the group, Yazidis are a peaceful people who often do not marry or interact regularly with those outside their own group. Their beliefs are derived from a combination of Zoroastrianism, Christianity, and Islam, and include baptism, religious respect for fire, and monotheism. Their religion is an ancient one linked to early Mesopotamian civilization and Sufism, but they have been persecuted throughout history on accusations of devil worship.

In 2014, ISIS took the city of Sinjar and other Yazidi areas in Iraq. Immediately, fighters began killing men, forcing women into slavery, and isolating children who could fight. Thousands of Yazidis fled to Mount Sinjar, where ISIS held them under siege for months without food or water. US, UK, and Kurdish forces were eventually able to push ISIS back and save those who were stuck while carrying out emergency drops of food and other goods. Since then, thousands of Yazidis have fled to Iraqi territory not held by ISIS, while others have been killed or enslaved by the group.

committed a mistake or evil,"[6] suggesting that it was being debated among the ranks. Despite this, the practice continues, and some support it wholeheartedly.

One man, who is not a member of ISIS but supports them, told Amnesty International in 2014 that he agrees with the group's outlook on the forced conversion of Yazidis and that he does not believe the women are enduring abuse, saying, "It is right and proper that these people [members of the Yazidi community] should convert to Islam and that the unmarried women should be married to Muslim men according to Islam. It is not true that they are oppressed, this is just propaganda. They are being fed and well treated like any other wives. I personally know some of the local men who have married these girls and they are good and honourable men."[7]

Many men are forced to join ISIS, but there are those who join voluntarily. Girl B, a Yazidi woman who has spoken to international organizations about her time as an ISIS hostage, explained that when ISIS arrived in the city of Sinjar, men she knew were quick to join them. "A local mechanic was among them. The Sunni men in our area became Daesh [the Arabic name for ISIS] as soon as they got a smell of them approaching. No one even had to ask them to join," she told the *Times*.[8] These men took part in the abduction of girls as young as fourteen, dragging them from their homes by their hair to be taken into slavery.

Of all the facts that Girl B has shared about her abduction and time with ISIS, this might be one of the most telling about how women fit into ISIS ideology: Hatred of women is a cornerstone of the group's treatment of women, and their permissive outlook on abuse allows some of the men who join them to act on their darkest, most twisted impulses.

In August 2014, thousands of Yazidi refugees were rescued from Iraq's Sinjar Mountains, where they had been stranded during fighting with ISIS. The new refugees were rescued by Kurdish Peshmerga soldiers who had been fighting against the Islamic State.

LIFE IN SLAVERY

For those who do become ISIS slaves, day-to-day life is totally upended. Young girls and teenagers are not offered education, and women are generally held in large houses until they are sold or forced to marry fighters. Thousands of women have been captured, including thousands of Yazidis, and the stories of those who escaped from ISIS territory show a harrowing existence.

Farida Khalaf is a Yazidi woman who lived in the village of Kocho in northern Iraq.[9] When ISIS arrived in 2014, Farida and other women who refused to convert to the group's particular style of Islam were forced into slavery and taken to Raqqa, where they were sold to men. The city is home to a modern-day slave market, where ISIS sells off women they take captive.

The same thing happened to Nehad, another Yazidi teenager who was taken captive and sold by ISIS in 2014. She was sold to multiple fighters, eventually being forced to live with one militant and his wife, where she became pregnant.

"It's difficult to see what ISIS do and hear what they're capable of, because I think the reality is so much worse than what the world thinks of them," Nehad told *Buzzfeed* in 2016. "I find it hard to swallow, to cope with—they're allowed to get away with it, and grow, and do whatever they want."[10]

Nadia Murad Basee Taha, another Yazidi woman from Kocho, has become an international advocate for bringing ISIS to justice. She has testified at the United Nations and has become one of the most outspoken figures who has lived through the horror of ISIS. She told *Time* in 2015 that when she and the other women from her village were taken by ISIS, many women tried to make themselves less attractive by putting battery acid on their faces, while others attempted to kill themselves.[11]

Nadia and the other women being held with her were passed between fighters, beaten, and raped. Some women in their position killed themselves rather than risk being sold or forced into marriage. Luna, a twenty-year-old woman, told Amnesty International about a fellow prisoner named Jilan who chose death over forced marriage:

> "We were 21 girls in one room, two of them were very young, 10-12 years. One day we were given clothes that looked like dance costumes and were told to bathe and wear those clothes. Jilan killed herself in the bathroom. She cut her wrists and hanged herself. She was very beautiful. I think she knew that she was going to be taken away by a man and that is why she killed herself."[12]

3

GENDER VIOLENCE IN

ISIS TERRITORY

Violence is part of everyday life under ISIS rule, for both men and women. It is used as a tool to instill fear and force those in ISIS's territory to abide by its laws and regulations. But for women, violence is compounded by expectations of how women will behave, a lack of personal freedom, and the total control of their husbands. ISIS has created a system that makes gender violence part of its institutions, and that allows women to be abused and victimized repeatedly.

Gender violence is defined as abuse, be it sexual, physical, or in some cases emotional, against women based on their gender. It is a widespread problem around the world, but ISIS has taken it to new levels by formalizing slavery and creating an education system that, if the group remains an influential power, could create a generation of women with few skills outside of the home. This is an institutional system that is designed to reinforce the notion that a woman's place is in the home and in service to her husband, and that her greatest contribution to society is her ability to have children.

Lamiya Aji Bashar, an eighteen-year-old Yazidi woman, was held captive by ISIS soldiers, used as a sex slave, beaten, and raped. Bashar was injured by a landmine exploding during her escape.

WOMEN HELD HOSTAGE

ISIS has institutionalized sexual slavery and assault, and the women who have escaped their captivity have explained the systematic way in which ISIS captures, holds, and sells women. It begins when ISIS takes control of a village; first it separates men from women, and then young unmarried women from the rest. These women and girls are high priority for selling or forcing into marriage. In most cases, all the women are taken to a city, like Raqqa or Mosul (before the city was retaken by Iraqi forces), where they are held in a house with other women.

All women held by ISIS are photographed and examined, then offered to fighters as either wives or slaves. In some cases, ISIS uses temporary marriages to allow fighters to assault women; some women who escaped ISIS reported being "married" more than twenty times in one weekend. Most women are moved multiple times, and some are passed from one man to another before either escaping or being chosen by one man to keep for a longer period of time.

One woman was held for over a month, along with her sister and other captives. She told Amnesty International about her time in captivity and the fate she believed awaited her if she hadn't managed to escape:

Hawain, a fourteen-year-old Yazidi girl, was captured and held for more than a month by ISIS militants. She eventually escaped to the Khanke refugee camp in Iraqi Kurdistan.

DIVORCE IN ISLAM

ISIS has rooted its teachings in an interpretation of Islam that is both very literal and twisted in complex ways. This is particularly true of marriage and divorce, both of which are used by the group to legitimize sexual assault and forced marriage. Temporary marriages (known as Mut'a) exist in Islam, but they are meant to be consensual, and the faith dictates that women who take part in temporary marriage should not enter another one for two months. Divorce is allowed in Islam and can be introduced by either the husband or wife. The religion has built into it mechanisms by which couples can divorce under Sharia, or Islamic legal teachings, although in most countries it falls under the government's control.

Under ISIS, both temporary marriages and divorce are used to formalize sexual assault. The group uses temporary marriages to "legalize" assault and then divorces the man and victim before immediately forcing her into another marriage. Women are in some cases able to file for divorce from their husbands but not in cases of abuse. Women can get a divorce under ISIS only when their husband will not join the group, making them an infidel under ISIS's teachings.

They kept bringing prospective buyers for us but luckily none of them took us because we are not beautiful and we were always crying and holding on to each other. We tried to kill ourselves and the man who was holding us promised not to separate us, but he was becoming more and more impatient. He wanted to get rid of us, to unload the responsibility for us on to someone else, and if we had not managed to escape it was only a matter of time before we would have ended up married by force or sold to some men, like many other girls.[1]

Women who are forced into slavery are considered the property of the men who buy them and have papers that essentially serve as deeds to them. Men can give them to others as gifts or sell the women if they want to, and some men buy multiple women and run businesses by selling them temporarily to other men. These women have no freedom of movement, have no access to the outside world, and in households are made to work alongside other slaves or wives.

Sexual violence is one of the most pervasive and well-understood forms of sexual violence that ISIS uses, particularly against women who are forced into slavery. Abuse and rape are used as punishment against women, but there are also reports that men believe that this abuse is sanctioned by their faith. In some cases, women have told researchers that their abusers prayed before or after assaulting them and that they were told their ongoing abuse was religiously encouraged.

Women who are not slaves are also restricted and in some ways held hostage. Their ability to work or leave the home is dependent entirely on their husbands. If their husbands do not want them to teach or work outside of the house, they cannot do so. Even for those who are able to leave the home, places to go and things to do are limited, and they run the risk of being

A propaganda photo released by the Islamic State shows ISIS soldiers posing with their weapons in Syria. Photos like this are used to recruit new members who want to participate in the violence the group promotes.

targeted by the morality police. A young man known as Samer shared day-to-day accounts of his life in Raqqa with BBC Radio 4 before they were published in 2017 in his book *The Raqqa Diaries*. He wrote about the abuse one woman suffered after her daughter misbehaved in public:

> The first time I saw the Hisbah, [ISIS's] religious police, patrolling the streets they were shouting at a woman

who was pulling her daughter back on to the pavement after the little girl had run into the road. The mother looked very decent, according to local standards anyway. She was wearing an abaya [loose-fitting, full-length robe] and a hijab, but they were calling her really bad names and questioning her honour because she wasn't wearing a face veil. They were using words that most of us would be too ashamed to say. How could they call themselves religious, I wondered. The young woman was becoming increasingly frightened and was trying to get away from them. She said she just wanted to take her daughter home, but they wouldn't leave her alone. By this time there were a few of us standing nearby; we were all shocked but didn't risk saying anything...[2]

FOREIGN WOMEN

There is some evidence that women who join ISIS from other countries have benefits, including greater internet access and more freedom of movement. Social media posts suggest that they are able to spend time outside on a regular basis, and their ability to update social media regularly suggests they have reliable internet and electricity, as well as the ability to go online as they wish.

Foreign women play an important role in ISIS's propaganda machine. According to the Quilliam Foundation, they provide firsthand verification of the supposed paradise ISIS promises to women who join them:

> Many of these Western female jihadists, who refer to themselves as muhaajirat—literally, immigrants—are very prominent on social media, be it Twitter, Facebook or Tumblr. There are at least 50 who have built a profile in this manner. They post incessantly, seemingly addicted to the limelight and attention. The internet helps them share the details of their new lives in the so-called Caliphate, adding to the adventurism and utopianism that permeates all of IS's recruitment propaganda. They tweet about weapons training and policing, implying that they fill leading positions in IS all-female brigades and units, stressing the great excitement of it all.[3]

While it could be possible that foreign women are not victims of the worst of ISIS's abuses, they are still aware that they take place. This creates a complex system in which women are given the power to victimize other women; this has been reported among former slaves or wives who have escaped. In some cases, fellow wives are equally as abusive as men, particularly those who join the morality police. Aisha, a woman who escaped ISIS territory, told Human Rights Watch about the punishments women doled out when she was arrested after trying to escape:

> She said that three female ISIS guards came and lashed each woman 65 times with a thin cane, saying that if they even winced, they would get more lashes.[4]

Another young woman who escaped Raqqa told the news website Syria Deeply that during her detention a woman threatened her with a firearm, saying, "One of the women in the

Mannequins in a shop window in ISIS-controlled Mosul, Iraq, have their faces covered. Under ISIS rule, women are expected to wear full-face niqabs, or head scarves.

brigade came over, pointing her firearm at me. She then tested my knowledge of prayer, fasting, and hijab."[5]

What we know about the lives of foreign women who go to Syria to join ISIS is limited to what escaped women share and what is posted to social media, which is a heavily curated look at their day-to-day lives. It can be difficult to know, for example, if some foreign women are forced into marriage when their initial husbands, to whom these women are often married very quickly after arrival, are killed in battle. Very few foreign women return to their home countries after fleeing to join ISIS—in 2015, there were only two such women reported—and those who have will not speak publically due to pending legal action or the need to go into hiding.

THE NEXT GENERATION

For ISIS, raising the next generation of young people under its control is a crucial part of expanding its reach and furthering its ideology. In 2016, the Quilliam Foundation estimated that around 31,000 pregnant women were living in ISIS territory, and women's role in creating the next generation of fighters is a focus of ISIS propaganda and teaching. Indoctrination begins at an early age, with young boys being treated with extreme respect and encouraged to take part in trainings or even executions. Young girls are also taught from an early age that their role in society is that of raising devout children, serving their fighter husbands, and encouraging other women to live by ISIS commands.

Huda was starting high school when ISIS took control of Mosul. She saw firsthand how the group slowly rolled back education and changed the way girls could dress. "When ISIS

Madeline, a thirteen-year-old Yazidi girl, was ransomed by the Islamic State. After her family paid for her freedom, her mother cut her hair and dressed Madeline as a boy to prevent her from being taken again. Now, the family resides in a refugee camp in Northern Iraq with other escaped Yazidis.

WOMEN IN PROFESSIONS

Across Syria and Iraq, women have developed careers in fields like medicine, education, law, and other skilled professions. But when ISIS took control of the territories they now hold, the group moved to force women out of the workforce and into the home. Women, some of whom were able to work for a time, were harassed or forced out of their jobs and are unable to return to work outside of a few careers ISIS feels are appropriate, such as teaching children or working with the morality police.

But this has created issues. Chief among them is the medical situation. ISIS insists that male doctors not treat women, leading to a lack of resources for women in need of medical care. Although women are allowed to be doctors for other women, women who treat men in ISIS territory are threatened with punishment or death. Many clinics for women were closed by ISIS, and women doctors are required to comply with restrictive guidelines about clothing; they must cover their faces and hands, which makes surgery and procedures difficult. One female doctor who practiced in Raqqa under ISIS told the *IB Times*, "Every day I was subjected to their insults, names, everything...It's hard to even think about."[6]

came, they allowed us to go to school at first. But the dress code was black and long. Even the eyes should be hidden. They would always come to the school. It was scary, so then we left," she told Public Radio International in 2017. "They switched our science-based curriculums to the ISIS curriculum. It was all about murder."[7]

The Khansaa Brigade's guide to women under ISIS outlines the average education that girls should expect. From a young age, girls are taught few skills beyond those they will need to be wives and mothers, and girls should stop education around the age of sixteen rather than "flit here and there to get degrees and so on just so she can try to prove that her intelligence is greater than a man's." It says:

> From ages seven to nine, there will be three lessons: fiqh (understanding) and religion, Qur'anic Arabic (written and read) and science (accounting and natural sciences).
>
> From 10 to 12, there will be more religious studies, especially fiqh, focusing more on fiqh related to women and the rulings on marriage and divorce. This is in addition to the other two subjects. Skills like textiles and knitting, basic cooking will also be taught.
>
> From 13 to 15, there will be more of a focus on sharia, as well as more manual skills (especially those related to raising children) and less of the science, the basics of which will already have been taught. In addition, they will be taught about Islamic history, the life of the prophet and his followers.
>
> It is considered legitimate for a girl to be married at the age of nine. Most pure girls will be married by 16 or 17, while they are still young and active.[8]

Although taking away education is not violence in a traditional sense, it does contribute to the system that ISIS has created to keep women oppressed. By forcing young girls to end their education early to marry, ISIS is taking away crucial resources and skills that would otherwise be learned. At the same time, these young people are being forced to take on responsibilities far beyond their years, including motherhood. Pregnancy at too young an age can cause health issues and even prove fatal, and having young children can make it harder for these women to try to escape. If they are caught, their children will likely suffer alongside them, and if they leave their children behind, they will have to live fearing what became of them.

WHY WOMEN JOIN

ISIS

One of the many mysteries of ISIS is how it is able to successfully recruit fighters from around the world, but the group does the same with women. Although a majority of women are forced by ISIS to marry group fighters, some choose to join the group and travel to Syria or Iraq despite international regulations. Some countries have made it illegal to join ISIS, while others consider travel to its territory a form of support, another federal crime. Joining ISIS is immensely risky, and hundreds of people—including dozens of women—have been arrested attempting to go to Syria.

The reasons women join ISIS are complex, but most are rooted in isolation and manipulation. Through a complex system of radicalization, ISIS is able to find and prey on women who feel lonely or are vulnerable. The group has recruiters both in Syria and around the world, all of whom use social media to create a sense of community that encourages these women to isolate themselves from friends and family, identify with ISIS, and eventually join the group in Syria. Using propaganda and

A woman is seen outside The Hague in winter 2014, where four men were on trial for trying to recruit young Muslims to go to Syria to fight with the Islamic State. Because of how difficult it is to track these militants, very few supporters have been held accountable for their actions in support of ISIS.

promoting an image of "sisterhood" among ISIS wives, they have been able to convince hundreds—if not thousands—of women to travel to ISIS territory and swear allegiance to al-Baghdadi's leadership.

HOW ISIS RECRUITS WOMEN

Radicalization is a complex process that can take months to complete, but it is also something we often associate with men who become terrorist fighters. For women, the process is no less long and complicated. ISIS tends to prey on vulnerable people who are socially isolated or looking for meaning in their lives, particularly teens or young adults. While for men they promote heroism and courage, for women they focus more on how they can help further the fight by keeping the homes of fighters and the innate corruption of living under Western traditions. Instead, they say, come to Syria and live a truly Islamic life.

ISIS recruitment begins when a recruiter identifies someone who might be interested in joining the group. The recruit may have posted about being curious about ISIS, watched or shared a video from one of the many ISIS propaganda accounts, or otherwise engaged with someone linked to ISIS. In some cases, potential recruits also reach out to ISIS members, including some high-profile members known for being willing to speak to journalists or those who want to know more about the group.

In this image from security camera footage, three British girls who had run away to join ISIS in 2015 are shown at a bus station in Istanbul, Turkey, on their way to the Turkey-Syria border.

WHY ISIS TARGETS TEENAGERS

In recent years, ISIS has begun targeting teenagers as potential recruits. In 2015, three teenagers from London became famous when they were able to travel to Syria to join the group, and other teenagers or women in their early twenties have done the same. There are a few reasons why ISIS targets people at such a young age. One is that teenagers are often in search of meaning or community, and many feel isolated or misunderstood. ISIS is able to play on insecurity and make recruits feel they belong. This is true of both teenage boys and girls; boys are recruited as fighters and ISIS often leans on their sense of religious obligation to get them to join, while girls are recruited as brides, and often a softer tactic is taken to convince them that life under ISIS will benefit them. Teenagers and young women are less likely to have health problems that would make it difficult for them to have children, so they can help grow the group through childbirth. They are also easier to manipulate and control once they arrive in Syria, as they may not be aware of resources available to them if they escape ISIS territory. Because of this, teenagers are ideal recruits for the group and highly vulnerable to their techniques.

Once contact is made, the rest of the ISIS online network rallies around the potential recruit. While one person tries to interact daily via text message, social media account, or even Skype, hundreds of other ISIS members add the person across channels like Twitter or Facebook and encourage others to do the same. This creates an echo chamber, as well as a rush of friendship that many people find appealing. Because ISIS routinely targets teenagers or young adults who feel isolated, this influx of internet connections can have an immediate effect; the person begins to feel they have a community that they otherwise did not.

Over time, the recruiter and other members of ISIS will begin to encourage the recruit to take further steps. This could be joining ISIS in Syria if the recruit is already Muslim or encouraging non-Muslims to convert. They also encourage the recruit to begin living by ISIS regulations, including wearing strict hijab whenever they can and to pray regularly. Both men and women work to recruit women; men express a desire to marry the recruit, while women offer close friendship and support.

The final and most dangerous part of the process is encouraging the recruit to travel to Syria. The recruit could be in touch with ISIS for months or even close to a year by this point— it depends on the recruitment process and how the recruit responds. The group offers money, sending thousands of dollars to potential recruits to help them buy plane tickets. Recruits are encouraged to travel first to Turkey, then to a border area where they will either cross the border into Syria alone or after meeting with someone who will get them to ISIS territory. It is at this point that things become more volatile; many potential recruits are stopped before they even leave their own country, while others are stopped at airports on the way to Turkey or at the Syrian border. Some also decide to back out at the last minute due to concerns for their safety or the safety of those who are helping them travel.

In 2014, ISIS launched a program called Al-Zawra'a Foundation, which targets Western women who may be thinking about joining the group. It encourages women to learn domestic skills, like sewing or cooking, and to watch training videos before

ISIS relies heavily on social media to spread their message of hate and recruit new members. Because of the viral nature of social media posts, ISIS can reach people around the world.

coming to Syria. While it does not replace the immediate initial contact and earlier stages of recruitment, it does show that ISIS is working hard to bring women to its territory and encouraging them to develop certain skills that are valued by ISIS.

THE ROLE OF SOCIAL MEDIA

Social media is the key way that ISIS spreads propaganda and lures in women from around the world, with new accounts popping up faster than platforms can suspend them. In February

2016, Twitter deleted around 125,000 accounts associated with the group, but hundreds of thousands more exist. The group also uses more difficult-to-track sites like WhatsApp or Kik to communicate. It has a specific code it uses to communicate about plans to travel to Syria, adding to the sense of secrecy and inclusion that some women feel when joining ISIS. On sites like Twitter and Facebook, entire networks of women ISIS members have emerged that share a particularly empowering image of what the group stands for—namely girl power and sisterhood. This is a distorted image of ISIS, and one that doesn't take into account the widespread abuses in which the group engages.

The tactics for engaging with women on social media are varied; sometimes women members of ISIS reach out to people who seem interested, while other times men do so to promise marriage and swap romantic messages with potential brides. No matter how contact is made, anyone who seems interested in joining ISIS is immediately swamped by friend requests and followers, creating an echo chamber in which they hear nothing but positive things about ISIS. This also creates a sense of community, which is key for recruits who feel as if they are isolated. It allows ISIS to make them feel like they belong, and then use that sense of connection to lure them to the Middle East.

Hoda, a teenager from Alabama, joined ISIS in 2014 after gradually becoming more devout. She connected with ISIS members on social media and quickly replaced her circle of friends and peers with ISIS supporters. "I literally isolated myself from all my friends and community members the last year I was in America," she told *Buzzfeed* during a series of interviews from her home in Raqqa, Syria. "As I grew closer to my [faith], I lost all my friends, I found none in my community that desired to tread the path I was striving for."[1] The people she was

Although social media sites like Facebook, Twitter, and Instagram fight to rid their platforms of extremist messages, for every account deleted, dozens more spring up, keeping ISIS visible to anyone looking to find them online.

growing closer to eventually helped her travel from Alabama to Syria, where she married a fighter who was later killed in battle.

Women in ISIS territory post pictures and statuses that reflect a domestic life—shopping, cooking, and spending time with friends are common. Although they also sometimes post about bombings or jihad, more often they convey a sense of security that is strongly at odds with what we know about life under ISIS control. But these posts are used to create an image of a life that is at once filled with companionship and meaningful hardship. At the same time, women are welcomed into the *akhawat*, or sisterhood, and encouraged to join their new "sisters" in Syria.

HOW SOCIAL MEDIA SITES FIND ISIS ACCOUNTS

Given the wide reach and impact of social media accounts linked to ISIS, sites like Twitter and Facebook have actively worked to disable any they can find. The sites scrub huge numbers of accounts at once, sometimes close to 100,000 at a time. Although these users can and do set up new accounts quickly, on a site like Twitter, disrupting communication can break up the radicalization and recruitment process enough to delegitimize ISIS accounts. Studies have found that new accounts on Twitter rarely gain as many followers as previous accounts had, and since the site started targeting ISIS-linked accounts, the average number of tweets per day by pro-ISIS accounts dropped from close to nine at its highest to less than six in late 2015. Twitter uses a team of experts to analyze accounts identified by an algorithm to determine if someone is a member of ISIS or a potential recruit. The account is then monitored and eventually shut down or suspended. The exact specifics of the process are not known, due to concerns that too many details could allow ISIS to find a workaround.

Women's posts on social media are also laced with violence, and pictures of children with guns are common. So are messages about the importance of marriage and having children, both of which are presented to readers as both duties and privileges. At the same time, posts about the loss of fathers in battle are equally as common, along with calls for women to see this not as a loss but as a chance for their children to follow in their fathers' footsteps. The combined image of life under ISIS that these messages creates—devoted marriage, motherhood, and eventually being widowed—is in line with what we know about the arc a woman's life is expected to take under ISIS.

ISIS PROPAGANDA VS. REALITY

Journalist Anna Erelle, who has written numerous pieces about ISIS, was able to pose as a potential recruit during conversations with an ISIS fighter named Bilel in 2014. During an early Skype conversation—their first—he made clear what he hoped would come of their conversation, saying, "Listen, Melodie [a fake name Erelle used], among other things, it's my job to recruit people, and I'm really good at my job. You can trust me. You'll be really well taken care of here. You'll be important. And if you agree to marry me, I'll treat you like a queen."[2]

Erelle, as Melodie, spoke with Bilel for weeks, eventually hatching a plot to go as far as she could safely to understand how the recruitment process works. This meant pretending she would go to Syria and marry him, when in fact she meant to only go so far as the Turkish border. But at the last minute the plan changed, and Bilel told her to buy a ticket to Urfa, a city in southeastern Turkey, where ISIS was active. When Erelle (and the fake friend she claimed to be traveling with) became concerned, the true nature of Bilel—who had been kind and gentle—came out:

"Do you think I'm an idiot? From now on, you're going to shut up. I'm part of a terrorist organisation. You can't talk to me like that. Don't you know who I am? I command 100 soldiers every day. I haven't even told you a quarter of the truth. I'm wanted internationally; that's why I can't even go to our cities in Turkey. I can only travel to Iraq. I'm 38, and you and your friend can't bring me down. You'd better tread lightly."[3]

When Erelle told him that she had decided to go back to France, claiming that a man had questioned her and made her believe she was being watched, Bilel had a chilling response: "You're going to pay."

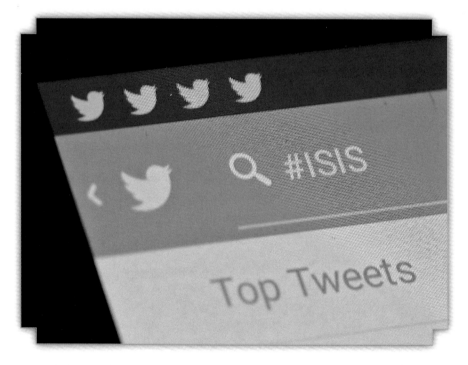

ISIS followers frequently hijack popular hashtags on Twitter to spread their own message, forcing anyone looking at a trending topic to see ISIS propaganda.

What Erelle experienced is a good example of the reality women face versus the treatment they expect when arriving. Although recruiters do make clear that there is struggle involved, they often sugarcoat or gloss over concerns about human rights abuses in favor of a utopian vision of an Islamic society—which the young women and girls who join them will have a hand in building. But when these women arrive, they are faced with repression and isolation, and the fear that if they change their minds or step out of line, ISIS could execute them or maim them as punishment.

But what makes it especially difficult to undermine the messages coming from female recruiters online is that little is known about the lives of foreign women in ISIS territory beyond what ISIS members share. One example of this disconnect is the story of Sterlina Petalo, an eighteen-year-old from the Netherlands who traveled to Syria in 2014 to marry a fighter named Omar "Israfil" Yilmaz. Petalo had been active on social media, but in March of 2014, she went silent after her divorce from Yilmaz. Although he has told Western media outlets that they split peacefully and she has since remarried, conflicting reports emerged that she was abused and possibly forced into sexual slavery. Petalo was eventually reunited with her mother later that year, but the months of silence highlight the fact that for women who join ISIS, the threat of disappearing is very real.

STORIES OF

ESCAPE

5

For women living under ISIS, life is dominated by fear and control. Their movements are heavily restricted, with some unable to leave the house and others forced to be slaves with no say in how they go about their day. But despite the general atmosphere of being monitored and observed at all times, many brave women have escaped ISIS territory. The harrowing journey could be deadly if they are found by ISIS, and many are forced to leave behind children or other family members. But given ISIS's use of violence and terror, for these women, the choice is literally life or death.

Escaping ISIS can be done in several ways. In most cases, women see an opportunity to get away and take it, traveling huge distances before crossing into non-ISIS territory. In some cases, women are helped by others within ISIS who can provide papers that allow them to travel within ISIS territory and get to safety. There are also organized efforts to save women, with people risking their lives to bring groups of women to safety. Although the stories are all different, the journeys are similarly laced with fear, danger, and the will to survive.

THOSE WHO FLEE

ISIS is a group in which men hold all power; women are not protected from abuse, sexual assault, or restrictions on their movement or activities. This is the root of why many women decide to escape—their lives are dominated by pain and suffering. But it is also why escaping is so difficult for so many. Women who are caught are subjected to punishments ranging from beatings to slavery, and in some cases the families of those who escape are punished as well.

Qaliya, a Yazidi woman who was abducted in 2014, was twenty-one when she told photojournalist Seivan M. Salim about her first attempted escape from ISIS. Her story highlights the dangers that women who flee face; being caught can mean harsh punishments that could be fatal:

> When I was in Mosul I tried to flee by running to Sinjar mountain. I found a small empty house, where I sat and waited, but they came looking for me and they found me. A man asked, "Why did you flee? Are you afraid that we will kill you?" I replied that I preferred to die. They took me back to my captor's house, where he pushed me inside a room, closed the door and started to whip me. After that he hit me with a cable and then fastened my

Yazidi refugees gather at a camp on Iraq's Mount Sinjar, in Iraq. ISIS has specifically targeted the minority Yazidi population because of their religious beliefs and the fact that the Yazidi community is small and insular, making it an easy target.

legs and hung me by the legs to the fan on the ceiling and then started to hit me again. He took me down and told me that my punishment would continue for three days and I would have nothing to eat nor drink. He also told me that if I ran away again he would tie me to two cars and then split me in two. Three days later he let me out of the room.[1]

Salim interviewed several Yazidi women who escaped ISIS, and their stories are diverse. Perla, another twenty-one-year-old, was one woman who saw a chance and took it:

> At night I tried to escape from the main door but it did not open. The side door did though. I wore the black abay and run away. I found some taxis and got into one asking the driver to take me to see my uncle at the border with Turkey. An ISIS car stopped the taxi and questioned the man and myself. They asked me what I was doing alone, without children outside the house. Then the taxi driver told the men that my uncle had an accident and he was helping me to get to him. They let us go, and the man drove me to Tel Abyad at the border with Turkey, where I was rescued.[2]

Stories like Perla's are numerous. For many women, it takes several key elements to come together at once to make their escape possible. First, they have to have a moment when they are not being watched, such as when they are alone at home. They also have to contend with the authorities and present a plausible reason why they would be outside of the home by themselves. Another interviewee, named Nasima, was also able

Kurdish and Yazidi women chant and sing anti-ISIS slogans during a protest against the extremist group. Yazidi women are disproportionately targeted by ISIS for enslavement.

to rely on a taxi driver to help her; after escaping the man she was forced to marry, she got into a cab and told him she was fleeing a life of slavery. Rather than turn her in, he helped her contact her brother and arrange for a smuggler to get her out of ISIS territory.

OPPOSITION TO ISIS

ISIS is known for its violence against those who defy it. But this has not stopped some within its territory from working hard to save women living in unthinkable conditions. This resistance can take many forms. Smugglers who charge thousands of dollars to help women escape work across ISIS territory with those who have families capable of paying for their services, while networks of people who communicate via cell phone also exist.

One of these groups was created by Yazidis with contacts in ISIS territory. They include informants among the bureaucracy and Muslims who are willing to serve as an "underground railroad" for Yazidis and others in need. Organized by former lawyer Khalil al-Dakhi, the network helps women communicate with the outside world and arrange their escape. He told WNYC in 2015 that it can sometimes take up to a month to save a family or individual.

Individuals also play a large role in making it possible for women to escape. Whether it's civilians living under ISIS who want to make a difference or other women who use their power to help those escaping, these people are equally as brave as the women they help. ISIS has carried out mass executions of people who have helped women flee, making examples of these people by beheading them in public.

For most women, being bought or forced into marriage to ISIS fighters means a continuation of the horrors they have experienced. But in some cases, some women have reported being helped by members of ISIS or their wives. This is a huge risk for those who decide to help captives; escaping ISIS territory can carry a death sentence for those who are caught, and ISIS uses these kinds of punishments to make an example of those who violate the rules.

A young Yazidi woman was among thousands of Yazidis who had to flee Iraq when ISIS took control of parts of the country. A number of Yazidis escaped to Turkey to find safety.

Although these stories are rare, they offer a glimpse at how women within the caliphate subvert and undermine the group's more horrific teachings by giving young captives some element of security and even risking their own lives to see them to safety. One thirteen-year-old who was living with her captor was not only spared the abuse many women go through but was ultimately saved by him. She told Amnesty International:

> He took me to his home and I slept in a room with his older wife while he slept in another room with his younger wife. The older wife was very nice to me. He said he had bought me because he felt sorry for me and wanted to send me and my little sister back to my family and indeed he did so.[3]

Some women who were bought by foreign fighters told Amnesty International that the men's wives used their privileges as foreign women to help the young girls communicate with their families and made it possible for the girls to escape. One such girl told Amnesty International, "She was more than a mother to us. I could never forget this woman, she saved our lives."

Maysa, who spoke to Salim when she was eighteen years old, was sold to a man who caught her trying to escape. He beat her with a cable and told her that if she did not agree to marry him he would sell her to a man who was even more abusive. But when he left the house the following day, his wife intervened:

> [She] told me that she could help me escape to a Kurdish family living in the neighborhood. She took me there when her husband was out and I asked the Kurdish family to help me, I begged them. I stayed with them for five months. Then one day we could finally arrange with my father to meet at the border with Turkey. The Kurdish man gave me his daughter's ID and drove me to the border, where I was finally rescued.[4]

Jinan, a young Yazidi woman, was captured by ISIS and forced into sexual slavery by the militant Islamic group. While Jinan eventually escaped to freedom, untold numbers of Yazidi women remain captives of ISIS.

According to one family, they were not the only ones who wanted to help a young Yazidi woman, but they were the only ones who did so. Arezu was just twenty when she was forced into slavery and sold to a man who did not assault her, but nonetheless kept her hostage in his home. When the neighbors, a Syrian Muslim family, heard her crying and yelling, they decided to do something to help her. They told the *Guardian* in 2015 that they pretended to be interested in buying Arezu to marry her to one of their brothers. But when they finalized the deal, the family instead worked tirelessly to help her contact her family and plan her escape. They eventually got her out of the country

SMUGGLERS

Human smugglers have become a growing industry in the Middle East as ongoing conflicts and extremist groups force millions to flee their homes. These people are often paid thousands of dollars to get people where they hope to go, be it out of ISIS territory or all the way to Europe. But they are also dangerous; many do not follow safety guidelines, and hundreds have died crossing the Mediterranean in dangerous boats that capsize or sink mid-journey. For women and children in ISIS-held areas, these men can be a lifeline. For a fee, which can be paid in some cases by family members outside of the area, they help people escape across difficult terrain littered with checkpoints. Little is known about the smugglers, who must maintain anonymity to protect their safety, but some have suggested that they were helped by people with ties to ISIS, possibly people who are seeking to undermine the group or locals who are turning a profit.

The cost associated with escaping is part of what makes these individuals so mysterious; although some have spoken anonymously to the media and said they do this dangerous work for moral reasons, they are also making a fortune off the desperation of people in need. Nonetheless, hundreds—and perhaps thousands—have been saved via smuggling routes.

and back to her mother, who was in Turkey. Noor, one of the women in the family, said, "Our neighbors all wanted to do the same, but they didn't have the courage. When I think of this, I can't believe we did it."[5]

THOSE LEFT BEHIND

For women who do escape ISIS, moving forward is difficult for many reasons. Many of these women often have family or loved ones still living under ISIS, which haunts them. "I'm constantly reliving it, because it hasn't finished. My faith is helping me cope, but I'm still waiting for the rest of my siblings to be returned, and until they're home it continues to affect me. The pain has ripped my life and taken it over," Nehad told *Buzzfeed*.[6]

Whether they leave behind children, family members, or women they grew close to, these women are haunted by the fate of those whom they could not take with them. Muna, who spoke to Salim when she was eighteen years old, told her that five members of her family were still living under ISIS and she was unaware if they were still alive. Stories of families being punished for the escape of ISIS fighters or brides are common; in some cases, their homes are destroyed, they are beaten, or they are otherwise punished.

Randa was sixteen when ISIS abducted her and her family. Although she escaped soon after with one of her cousins, her family was left behind. She told Amnesty International in late 2014, "It is so painful what they did to me and to my family. Da'esh [ISIS] has ruined our lives. My mum gave birth while being held by Da'esh in Tal 'Afar; now she is being held in Mosul with my little sister and the baby. My 10-year-old brother was separated from my mum and is being held in Tal 'Afar with my aunt. What will happen to them? I don't know if I will ever see them again."[7]

بزکارهونا ته دا بی
جارنا منه
Y EID WILL BE WITH MY
M'S REALIZA

The abducted Ezidy
women and
girls are the honor
of all Kurds

رسالة أمل لأخواتي المختطفا
"نحن بأنتظاركن"

OPE MESSAGE TO MY

Yazidi women protest outside of the United Nations office in Erbil, Iraq, begging the UN to do something to help rescue the thousands of Yazidi women being held in slavery by ISIS.

LIFE AFTER ESCAPE

Women who escape ISIS face a difficult path to living their lives once again. Many have been subjected to severe physical abuse, and some are pregnant or have young children. Girls and adolescents who have been sexually assaulted are more likely to

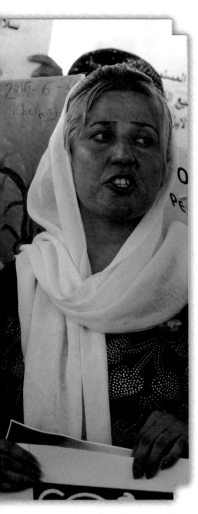

have lasting physical concerns that must be addressed, in addition to the mental toll such abuse takes on women young and old.

These women often live with symptoms of post-traumatic stress disorder, depression, anxiety, or other mental health issues that are difficult to address in the temporary refugee camps some of them live in. In countries like Iraq, where hundreds of women have found refuge, the mental health care system is already strained and has proven unable to keep up with the needs of women who have faced daily torture and abuse. According to Dr. Ali Muthanna, who works with Amar International Charitable Foundation in Iraq, the range of mental health issues these women live with is wide and often physical:

All too often we see cases of girls suffering from severe depression, crippling anxiety, panic attacks, headaches and nausea. Some self-harm, and many struggle to maintain relationships. Children frequently suffer from terrifying nightmares and struggle to communicate and concentrate—signs that their subconscious is grappling with memories of brutal violence.[8]

Rothna Begum of Human Rights Watch spoke with Yazidi women who had escaped and were seeking help in refugee camps. One girl, called Noor, had been sold to men who beat and sexually assaulted her for five days. She and a friend

SERVICES IN REFUGEE CAMPS

The international community is currently dealing with a refugee crisis, with more than twenty million refugees currently displaced, and millions more displaced within their home countries due to war, persecution, or famine. ISIS has contributed significantly to that number, with millions fleeing its territory. That number continues to increase as more and more people are able to get away from ISIS, but when they escape they find themselves entering an already-strained system that struggles to deal with the complex needs of refugees. For women who have been assaulted, mental and physical care must be provided, and many carry deep shame or guilt about what happened to them while being held. Young people have often missed years of education or endured trauma that makes returning to the learning environment difficult. Although groups like Human Rights Watch, the United Nations High Commissioner for Refugees, and governments that host these refugees do their best with limited resources, refugee camps are poor places for women dealing with the impact of prolonged abuse, fear, and control.

ultimately were able to escape while the men were away. By the time Rothna and her co-researcher Samer Muscati arrived at the camp, Noor had gone through a long healing process that was helping her get back on her feet:

> When she first came to the camp, she looked like a ghost, people told us. She was reunited with her parents, who were traumatized after their only son, Noor's brother,

Yazidi children pose for a photo in Sinjar, Iraq, where thousands of Yazidis were stranded during fighting between Kurdish peshmerga and ISIS militants. Approximately fifty thousand Yazidis took refuge on Mount Sinjar to escape the fighting.

was executed in front of them. But Noor had her parents' support. She said that she'd been to the hospital a few times, is receiving regular counseling, and is taking a sewing class. Her friend that she escaped with lives in a separate camp, and her father has taken her there to visit. Sometimes NGO activists take her out of the camp for social activities like going to the mall. She says she still has nightmares, but she's healing. She's going to be someone who can identify herself as a survivor, not just as a victim.[9]

6

LOOKING

AHEAD

The story of women under ISIS has so far been grim, violent, and abusive. But that is only part of the story. Women are on the forefront of stopping ISIS, using many different approaches to bring the group to justice and to save the women who are still living in its territory. From former slaves or brides to international human rights lawyers, women are leading the way as the international community tries to confront ISIS.

WOMEN HELPING WOMEN

Women who have escaped ISIS live with complex physical and mental concerns that take years to overcome. But even so, many have decided to channel their energy toward helping those who are still living under ISIS. One woman who was abducted from Kocho and forced into sexual slavery told the Global Fund for Women that she wants to make a difference for those still in ISIS captivity. "I would like to do something for my people. We are a kind people, we are a closed religion. We don't do any harm, we don't proselytize. Yet we have no one protecting us,

Nadia Murad, a twenty-two-year-old Yazidi woman, was held captive and forced into slavery by ISIS militants. She now works as an advocate for other women being held in slavery.

we are attacked for our faith and because we are not Muslim," she said.[1]

There are a number of groups organized by women or relying on women to help those who are in need. The Organization of Women's Freedom in Iraq is a non-governmental organization that has added programs for women fleeing ISIS to its long

Two women from the Kurdish People's Protection Unit, or YPG, sit with their guns at a camp outside Kobane, Syria. The women of the YPG are some of the fiercest fighters on the front lines of the battle against ISIS.

list of women-focused services. Founded by female activist Yanar Mohammed, the group works to combat gender violence and discrimination in Iraq, and operates centers to provide support and education to young Yazidi women and others who have endured life under ISIS. Prior to the center opening, Mohammed told *Huffington Post*, "In collaboration with the

Yazidi community, OWFI is setting up Yazidi Women's Empowerment Center in the Qadiya Camp, where sessions of psycho-social support will be provided to the women by Yazidi doctors and psychiatrists. The center will also provide support for the women in their daily lives. We in OWFI continue to open safe houses and centers for empowering our sisters who were victimised."[2]

WADI, an Iraqi-German non-governmental organization, uses mobile units made up of women to help Yazidis fleeing ISIS. These groups have many members who have fled ISIS themselves, giving them a keen understanding of what these women need and are going through. The women on the teams travel to isolated Yazidi communities that have developed as groups flee and provide support to the men and women they find there. Along with clothing and other basic goods, the women provide counseling, arrange medical care, and help them get access to resources. They also provide emotional support and stability, which can be life-changing for women or girls who have known years of hardship. The group's founder, Thomas von der Osten-Sacken, told *NBC News*, "A lot of [their cases] are now very eager to study, to learn, to do something. You need a future. You cannot always be pulled back in your own terrible past."[3]

In areas that have been liberated from ISIS, women are also taking a lead role in ensuring that their freedoms are respected by the community. All-women police units have emerged in cities in Syria, and in Manjib, a city that was liberated in 2016 after two years under ISIS control, women organized a political council to promote gender equality and women's rights.

FIGHTING ISIS

While many women have chosen to help from outside ISIS territory, some women have chosen to take up arms against their former abusers. One is the Kurdish Women's Protection Units (YPJ), a group of women who have taken the lead in physically retaking ISIS territory. At several thousand strong, the group is playing a key role in the fight against ISIS. The YPJ played a crucial role in saving the many Yazidis who were stranded on Mount Sinjar after the city of Sinjar was taken in 2014, and they fought alongside male units to liberate the city of Kobani. Evin Ahmed, a member of the YPJ, told *Marie Claire* that she took up arms because the Syrian government couldn't protect Kurds or other minorities from ISIS: "They can't protect us from [ISIS], we have to protect us [and] we defend everyone… no matter what race or religion they are."[4]

In recent years, other all-female units have been inspired by the YPJ. In 2015, the Bethnahrain Women's Protection Forces were founded to protect Assyrian and Syriac women and other vulnerable populations against not only ISIS but any group that seeks to harm women. The group was also part of the efforts to retake Raqqa from ISIS, which began in late 2016. The announcement of its founding read in part:

ISIS started a cultural, ethnic and denominational war against Christians, Yazidis, Alevis, defenders of democracy and reformers. This corrupted mindset lives in Mosul, Sengal, Nineveh Plain, Kobane Khabar Al Karyatayn and many more places. ISIS, Al Qaeda, Boko Haram, Al Shabab, Al Nusra and their inhuman organizations aim to enslave women forever, destroy democracy and foul the core of societies. That's why people who have empathy and sympathy and especially women should struggle against ISIS and its supporters.[5]

In late 2016, the Syrian Democratic Forces' al-Bab Military Council introduced an all-female unit, made up of Syrian women, many of whom had fled ISIS. The group is named for al-Bab, a city in northern Syria that was invaded by ISIS. Women who have lived under ISIS decided to join the group

PESHMERGA

The Peshmerga are Kurdish forces that have been on the forefront of fighting ISIS in Syria. Operating largely in Iraqi Kurdistan, the Peshmerga are governed by the Democratic Party of Kurdistan and the Patriotic Union of Kurdistan, and headed by the president of Iraqi Kurdistan. The word "peshmerga" means "one who confronts death," a fitting name for the fighters who have been engaging ISIS directly since 2014. The group has played a role in almost every major battle with ISIS, including the retaking of Mosul and Sinjar. Women make up a significant portion of fighters among the Peshmerga, and their work against ISIS has been covered extensively by the media.

to fight against their abusers, with one saying, "An ISIS female jihadi was responsible for torturing me in a very brutal way. And now I've joined the al-Bab Military Council in order to fight those terrorists."[6]

The Yazidis are also getting in on the fight. The Sun Ladies Brigade is an all-female group of fighters who are based in Iraqi Kurdistan. The Yazidi faith is not one with a strong combat tradition, and killing is forbidden by its religious teachings. But women who have been assaulted, lost their husbands and families, and been driven from their homes decided the need to defeat ISIS was too great to step aside. Khatoon Khider, a commander in the Sun Ladies, told *Vogue*, "Our history is dark. What happened to us is unthinkable...If ISIS killed your men and raped your sisters and your mothers and your friends, you would do the same."[7]

These female fighting forces play a crucial role in beating back ISIS and retaking territory, but they also play an important symbolic role in the fight. Given the oppression ISIS uses against women, to have women on the frontlines against them is an empowering counter-narrative to the one ISIS insists women follow. Rather than waiting to be saved or liberated, women are taking charge and saving their fellow women from an organization that does not value or respect them.

THE INTERNATIONAL COMMUNITY

Women on the ground are making a huge difference in the fight against ISIS, but women are also championing international action. Nadia Murad Basee Taha has spoken at the United Nations on behalf of Yazidi women who have been targeted and abused by ISIS, and has worked closely with human rights lawyer Amal Clooney, a leading voice in encouraging the United Nations to hold ISIS accountable.

Human rights lawyer Amal Clooney is shown speaking at the United Nations in 2017. Clooney is working to bring ISIS to justice for the genocide of the Yazidi people.

"Calling it genocide is not enough," Clooney said. "Evidence needs to be gathered and the ISIS militants who committed these atrocities must be brought to court. It's ambitious, but when you look in these girls' eyes you realize it must be done."[8]

"Why it is taking so long?" Murad asked the United Nations during a meeting in early 2017. "I cannot understand why you are letting ISIS get away with it, or what more you need to hear before you will act. So today, I ask the Iraqi government and the UN to establish an investigation and give all the victims of Isis the justice they deserve."[9]

Clooney has advocated for the Security Council, the most powerful body at the United Nations, to take action to preserve evidence against ISIS, including witness statements and mass graves found in former ISIS territories. She has also called for the group to be referred to the International Criminal Court, a body that can prosecute war crimes and crimes against humanity.

But while advocating for women who are victims of ISIS is difficult, it is also difficult to know how to handle women who join the group voluntarily. We understand the process by which men are radicalized, and in some cases have been able to reverse the process. But for women who fall in love with fighters or even collaborate with ISIS to oppress others, the line between victim and criminal is heavily blurred. Ultimately, ISIS leadership bears the bulk of responsibility for crimes committed under its regime, but the international community must find a way to reckon with the role women have played in helping advance its control and enforce its rules.

THE FIGHT TODAY

The wide range of ways women are fighting ISIS highlights why this issue is so complex—there are many fronts on which

TRYING INTERNATIONAL CRIMES

The process by which crimes are tried by the International Criminal Court (ICC) is long, complex, and difficult, with many cases never formally going to trial. It begins when a state that has signed the Rome Statute asks the Office of the Prosecutor to investigate possible war crimes, or the UN Security Council refers a case to the court. The prosecutor then decides if the case warrants ICC action, after which an independent team of investigators is sent to gather evidence. Charges are brought against those who are most responsible for crimes, such as the leader of a government that used chemical weapons or a militia that used child soldiers. The ICC then issues an arrest warrant, which cannot be carried out unless a state agrees to arrest and turn the accused over to the court, which does not have its own police force. This has proven tricky; arrest warrants sometimes stand for over a decade without action being taken. If the accused is arrested and taken to trial where they are found guilty, they can be sentenced with up to thirty years in prison, although in some cases life imprisonment is approved.

we have to make progress. No one part of the process is more important than another; it is crucial to combat recruitment, provide women with services, roll back ISIS's advances, and bring the group to justice. With so much to do, it has proven difficult to effectively combat the group, particularly as civil war rages in Syria.

As we have learned, women play a complex role in the advancement of ISIS ideology and are recruited in ways that differ from male recruits. Women living under ISIS are forced to endure abuse on a scale that few can fathom, and the women who join the group voluntarily present a complex set of concerns for the international community. But while women have been some of the main targets of ISIS's worst crimes, they are playing an important role in bringing the group to justice.

CHAPTER NOTES

Chapter 1: A History of ISIS

1. Tim Arango and Eric Schmitt, "U.S. Actions in Iraq Fueled Rise of a Rebel," *New York Times*, August 10, 2014, https://www.nytimes.com/2014/08/11/world/middleeast/us-actions-in-iraq-fueled-rise-of-a-rebel.html?_r=0.

2. Fazel Hawramy, Shalaw Mohammed, and Kareem Shaheen, "Life Under ISIS in Raqqa and Mosul: 'We're Living in a Giant Prison,'" *Guardian*, December 9, 2015, https://www.theguardian.com/world/2015/dec/09/life-under-isis-raqqa-mosul-giant-prison-syria-iraq.

3. Graeme Wood, "What ISIS Really Wants," *Atlantic*, March 2015, https://www.theatlantic.com/magazine/archive/2015/03/what-isis-really-wants/384980.

Chapter 2: Women in ISIS Ideology

1. Vivienne Walt, "Marriage and Martyrdom: How ISIS Is Winning Women," *Time*, November 18, 2014, http://time.com/3591943/isis-syria-women-brides-france.

2. Ruth Manning, "ISIL and Feminism," Quilliam Foundation, February 24, 2015, https://www.quilliaminternational.com/isil-and-feminism-by-ruth-manning.

3. Asadeh Moaveni, "ISIS Women and Enforcers in Syria Recount Collaboration, Anguish and Escape," *New York Times*, November 21, 2015, https://www.nytimes.com/2015/11/22/world/middleeast/isis-wives-and-enforcers-in-syria-recount-collaboration-anguish-and-escape.html.

4. Anonymous, "The Revival of Slavery: Before the Hour," *Dabiq*, Issue 4, https://clarionproject.org/docs/islamic-state-isis-magazine-Issue-4-the-failed-crusade.pdf (assessed May 26, 2017).

5. Kenneth Roth, "Slavery: The ISIS Rules," Human Rights Watch, September 5, 2015, https://www.hrw.org/news/2015/09/05/slavery-isis-rules.

6. Umm Sumayyah Al-Muhajirah, "Slave-Girls or Prostitutes?" *Dabiq*, Issue 9, https://clarionproject.org/

docs/isis-isil-islamic-state-magazine-issue+9-they-plot-and-allah-plots-sex-slavery.pdf (assessed May 26, 2017).

7. Amnesty International, "Escape From Hell: Torture and Sexual Slavery in Islamic State Captivity in Iraq," 2014, https://www.amnesty.org.uk/files/escape_from_hell_-_torture_and_sexual_slavery_in_islamic_state_captivity_in_iraq_-_english_2.pdf.

8. Anthony Lloyd, "Yazidi Girls Dragged by Their Hair into Sexual Slavery and Sold for $25," *Times*, December 22, 2014, https://www.thetimes.co.uk/article/yazidi-girls-dragged-by-their-hair-into-sexual-slavery-and-sold-for-dollar25-t0cqc8zxgsj.

9. Rachel Aspden, "The Girl Who Beat ISIS: My Story by Farida Khalaf and Andrea C. Hoffmann—review," *Guardian,* July 1, 2016, https://www.theguardian.com/books/2016/jul/01/the-girl-who-beat-isis-my-story-farida-khalaf-andrea-c-hoffman.

10. Rossalyn Warren, "How a 17-Year-Old Girl Is Trying to Regain Her Life After Escaping ISIS," *BuzzFeed*, April 4, 2016, https://www.buzzfeed.com/rossalynwarren/life-after-escape?utm_term=.tm6D3648w#.ifnnZ3zda.

11. Charlotte Alter, "A Yezidi Woman Who Escaped ISIS Slavery Tells Her Story," *Time*, December 20, 2015, http://time.com/4152127/isis-yezidi-woman-slavery-united-nations.

12. Amnesty International.

Chapter 3: Gender Violence in ISIS Territory

1. Amnesty International, "Escape From Hell: Torture and Sexual Slavery in Islamic State Captivity in Iraq," 2014, https://www.amnesty.org.uk/files/escape_from_hell_-_torture_and_sexual_slavery_in_islamic_state_captivity_in_iraq_-_english_2.pdf.

2. Samer, "The Raqqa Diaries: Life Under ISIS Rule," *Guardian*, February 26, 2017, https://www.theguardian.com/books/2017/feb/26/the-raqqa-diaries-life-under-isis-rule-samer-mike-thomson-syria.

3. Quilliam International, "Sisters in Arms: Why women fight for Islamic State," February 9, 2015, https://www.quilliaminternational.com/sisters-in-arms-why-women-fight-for-islamic-state.

4. Human Rights Watch, "Iraq: Sunni Women Tell of ISIS Detention, Torture," February 20, 2017, https://www.hrw.org/news/2017/02/20/iraq-sunni-women-tell-isis-detention-torture.

5. Ahmad al-Bahri, "In Raqqa, an All-Female ISIS Brigade Cracks Down on Local Women," *Syria Deeply*, July 15, 2014, https://www.newsdeeply.com/syria/articles/2014/07/15/in-raqqa-an-all-female-isis-brigade-cracks-down-on-local-women.

6. Lydia Smith, "Syrian Female Doctor Who Escaped Isis: 'Our lives in Raqqa turned to black,'" *International Business Times*, November 27, 2015, http://www.ibtimes.co.uk/syrian-female-doctor-who-escaped-isis-our-lives-raqqa-turned-black-1529368.

7. Richard Hall, "This Iraqi Woman Escaped ISIS and a Bad Marriage, All for the Love of her Children," *PRI*, January 23, 2017, https://www.pri.org/stories/2017-01-23/after-risking-death-save-her-children-isis-iraq-woman-refused-be-her-husbands.

8. Charlie Winter, trans., *Women of the Islamic State: A manifesto on women by the Al-Khanssaa Brigade*, February 2015, https://therinjfoundation.files.wordpress.com/2015/01/women-of-the-islamic-state3.pdf.

Chapter 4: Why Women Join ISIS

1. Ellie Hall, "Gone Girl: An Interview with an American in ISIS," *BuzzFeed*, April 17, 2015, https://www.buzzfeed.com/ellievhall/gone-girl-an-interview-with-an-american-in-isis?utm_term=.ib6Nkej5a#.fxWoJbwxB.

2. Anna Erelle, "How One Journalist Found Herself Courted by ISIS," *Vogue*, June 2, 2015, http://www.vogue.com/article/in-the-skin-of-a-jihadist-isis-recruitment-network-excerpt-anna-erelle.

3. Anna Erelle, "Skyping with the Enemy: I went undercover as a jihadi girlfriend," *Guardian*, May 26, 2015, https://www.theguardian.com/world/2015/may/26/french-journalist-poses-muslim-convert-isis-anna-erelle.

Chapter 5: Stories of Escape

1. Seivan M. Salim, "The Yazidi Women Who Escaped ISIS," *Daily Beast*, 2015, http://www.thedailybeast.com/longforms/2015/isis/portraits-of-the-yazidi-women-who-escaped-isis.html.

2. Ibid.

3. Amnesty International, "Escape From Hell: Torture and Sexual Slavery in Islamic State Captivity in Iraq," 2014, https://www.amnesty.org.uk/

files/escape_from_hell_-_torture_and_sexual_slavery_in_islamic_state_
captivity_in_iraq_-_english_2.pdf.

4. Seivan M. Salim.

5. Emma Graham-Harrison, "'You Will Stay Here Until You Die': One
   woman's rescue from Isis," *Guardian*, December 26, 2015, https://www
   .theguardian.com/world/2015/dec/26/arezu-yazidi-woman-rescued-
   isis-neighbours-raqqa.

6. Rossalyn Warren, "How A 17-Year-Old Girl Is Trying To Regain
   Her Life After Escaping ISIS," *BuzzFeed*, April 4, 2016, https://www
   .buzzfeed.com/rossalynwarren/life-after-escape?utm_term=.tm6
   D3648w#.ifnnZ3zda.

7. Amnesty International.

8. Dr. Ali Muthanna, "Thousands Have Been Abused by Isis and Their
   Mental Health Is Shattered," *Guardian*, January 27, 2016, https://www
   .theguardian.com/global-development-professionals-network/2016/
   jan/27/islamic-state-yazidi-refugees-mental-health-treatment.

9. Amy Braunschweiger, "Interview: These Yezidi Girls Escaped ISIS. Now
   What?" Human Rights Watch, retrieved May 26, 2017, http://features
   .hrw.org/features/Interview_These_Yezidi_Girls_Escaped_ISIS/index
   .html.

Chapter 6: **Looking Ahead**

1. Jane Sloane, "Rozina's Story," Global Fund for Women, https://www.
   globalfundforwomen.org/refugee-crisis-rozinas-story/#.WPg6yseSXzI
   (assessed May 26, 2017).

2. Eve Ensler, "An Interview with Iraqi Women's Leader Yanar
   Mohammed of the Organization for Women's Freedom in Iraq,"
   Huffington Post, http://www.huffingtonpost.com/eve-ensler/an-
   interview-with-iraqi-w_b_8332170.html (assessed May 26, 2017).

3. James Novogrod, "Aid Workers Help Yazidi Women Return to Life After
   ISIS Nightmare," *NBC News*, February 17, 2015, http://www.nbcnews
   .com/storyline/isis-uncovered/aid-workers-help-yazidi-women-return-
   life-after-isis-nightmare-n307206.

4. Elizabeth Griffin, "These Remarkable Women Are Fighting ISIS. It's
   Time You Know Who They Are," *Marie Claire*, October 30, 2014,
   http://www.marieclaire.com/culture/news/a6643/these-are-the-
   women-battling-isis.

5. BIA News Desk, "Bethnahrin Women Protection Forces Founded Against ISIS," September 2, 2015, http://bianet.org/english/women/167293-bethnahrin-women-protection-forces-founded-against-isis.

6. Simon Robb, "Syrian Women Have Set Up Their Own Female-Only Battalion to Fight Isis," *Metro*, November 2, 2016, http://metro.co.uk/2016/11/02/syrian-women-have-set-up-their-own-female-only-battalion-to-fight-isis-6229049.

7. Janine di Giovanni, "How Yazidi Women Are Fighting Back Against ISIS," *Vogue*, October 26, 2016, http://www.vogue.com/article/sun-ladies-yazidi-women-isis-genocide-sexual-enslavement.

8. Ibid.

9. Edith M. Lederer, "Amal Clooney: Don't let Islamic State get away with genocide," *Associated Press*, March 10, 2017, http://bigstory.ap.org/article/6610ef724bad4d7ebc44a287ba0cd63e/amal-clooney-dont-let-islamic-state-get-away-genocide.

GLOSSARY

abaya A loose fitting black dress worn by some Muslim women and required in countries like Saudi Arabia.

affiliates Groups that have pledged allegiance to a larger organization and operate with loose connections to that organization.

caliphate A political and religious state governed by Islamic law and ruled by a caliph.

devout Deeply religious, with religious beliefs guiding most behaviors or decisions.

ethnic cleansing The deliberate use of force or intimidation to make a group leave an area, whether through mass extermination or forced relocation.

excommunicate Cast out of a religion.

fanaticism Religious devotion that becomes so extreme that it results in behaviors that are dangerous or otherwise outside the norm.

hijab Can refer to the religious practice of covering some part of the face, head, or body or the headscarf some women wear.

ideology The central beliefs that guide a person's choices or a group's goals.

insurgent A rebel that uses guerrilla warfare tactics to target an institution, such as an occupying military or a government.

Islamic Empire A collective term for numerous empires that controlled the modern Middle East, North Africa, and at times parts of Spain and Turkey.

militant Using extreme tactics or violence to advocate for a political or social cause.

millenarian A religious belief in the coming of the end of the world.

niqab A face and hair covering that allows only an opening for the eyes, worn by Muslim women.

oppression The deliberate restriction of a person's or group's freedoms.

Ottoman Empire The last caliphate, with its government based in Turkey; it collapsed in 1924 following World War I.

al-Qaeda A terrorist organization once led by Osama bin Laden and based in Pakistan; it is considered a rival of ISIS.

Raqqa A city in Syria and the current de-facto capital of ISIS territory.

Salafism An extreme school of Sunni Muslim thought that advocates for a return to the ways of life associated with a strict and literal reading of Islamic texts.

Shia A branch of Islam that has been rejected by ISIS due to its willingness to embrace change and reformation of Islamic teachings.

Sunni A branch of Islam that traditionally does not have a religious hierarchy or uniform religious practices but emphasizes conservative readings of Islamic texts.

terrorism The use of violence and fear to achieve political goals.

Wahhabism Similar to Salafism but associated with the Saudi royal family and featuring a rejection of sects of Islam that accept or advocate reform.

FURTHER READING

Books

Atwan, Abdel Bari. *Islamic State: The Digital Caliphate.* Berkeley, CA: University of California Press, 2015.

Fawaz, Gerges A. *ISIS: A History.* Princeton, NJ: Princeton University Press, 2016.

Khalaf, Farida. *The Girl Who Beat ISIS: Farida's Story.* London, UK: Square Peg, 2016.

Samer. *The Raqqa Diaries: Escape from "Islamic State."* Northampton, MA: Interlink Books, 2017.

Websites

Council on Foreign Relations
www.CFR.org

Think-tank focusing on international affairs, with backgrounders and other information on ISIS.

Human Rights Watch
www.hrw.org

International human rights group with information and reports about the abuses taking place under ISIS.

INDEX